J 8A Gloster Gladiator

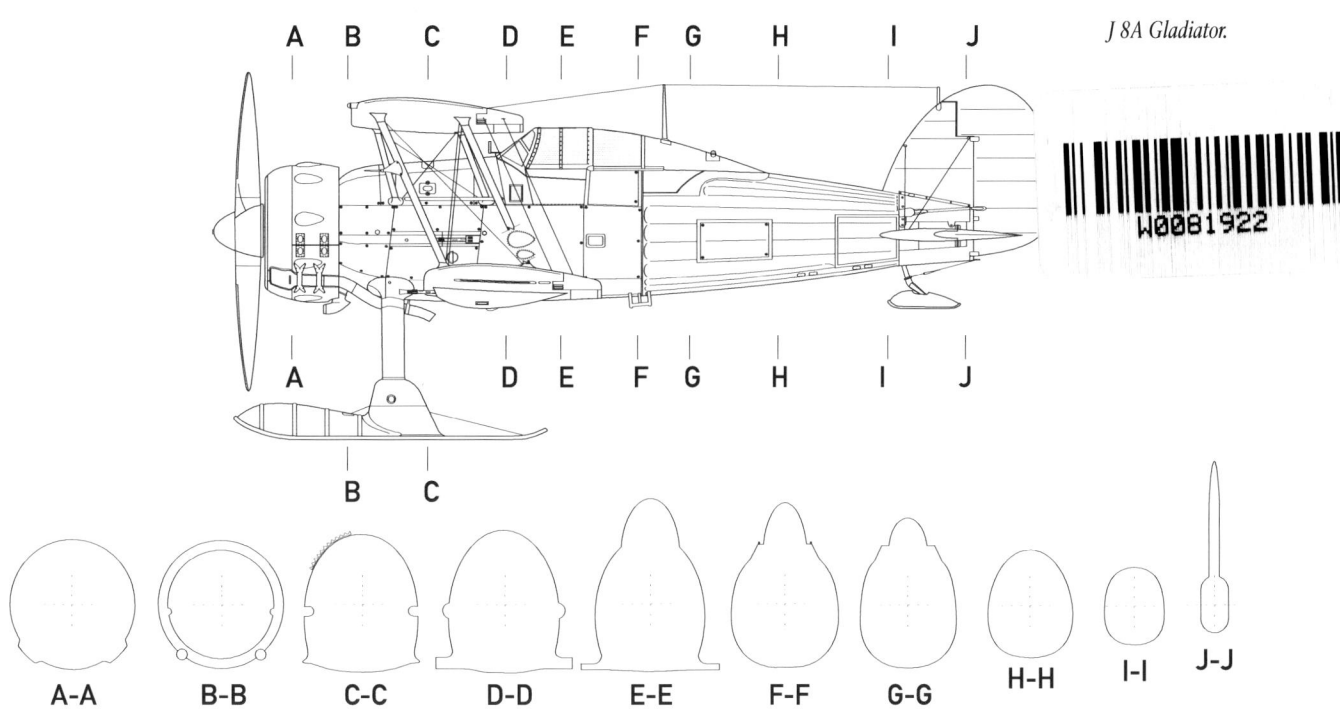

J 8A Gladiator.

A-A B-B C-C D-D E-E F-F G-G H-H I-I J-J

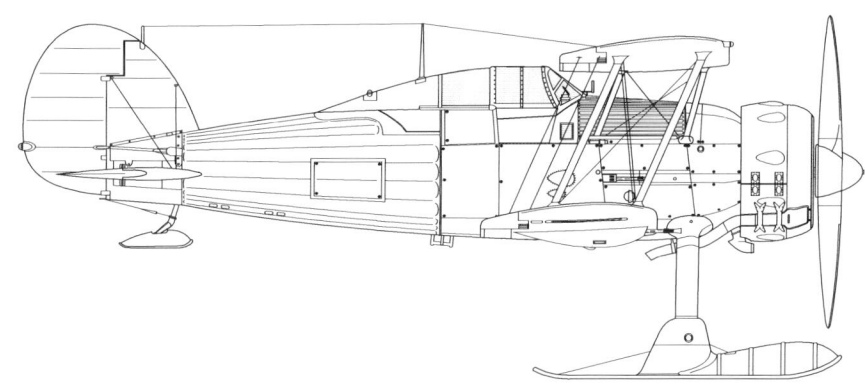

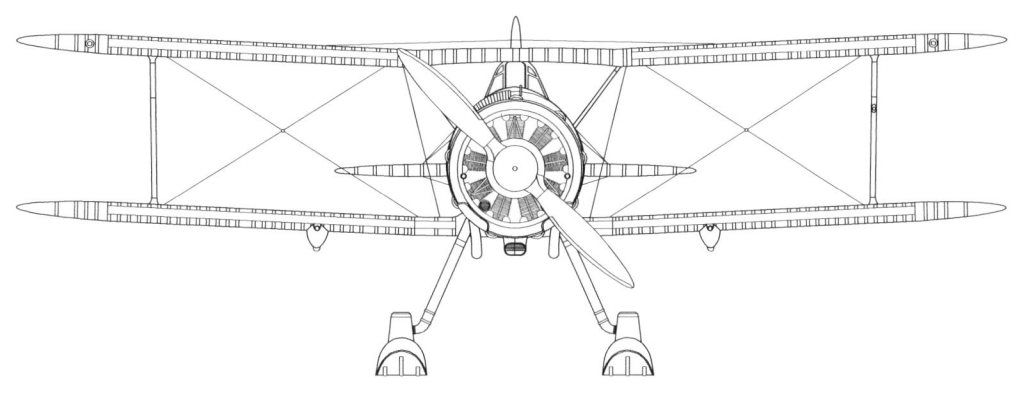

1/72

Drawings: Dariusz Karnas

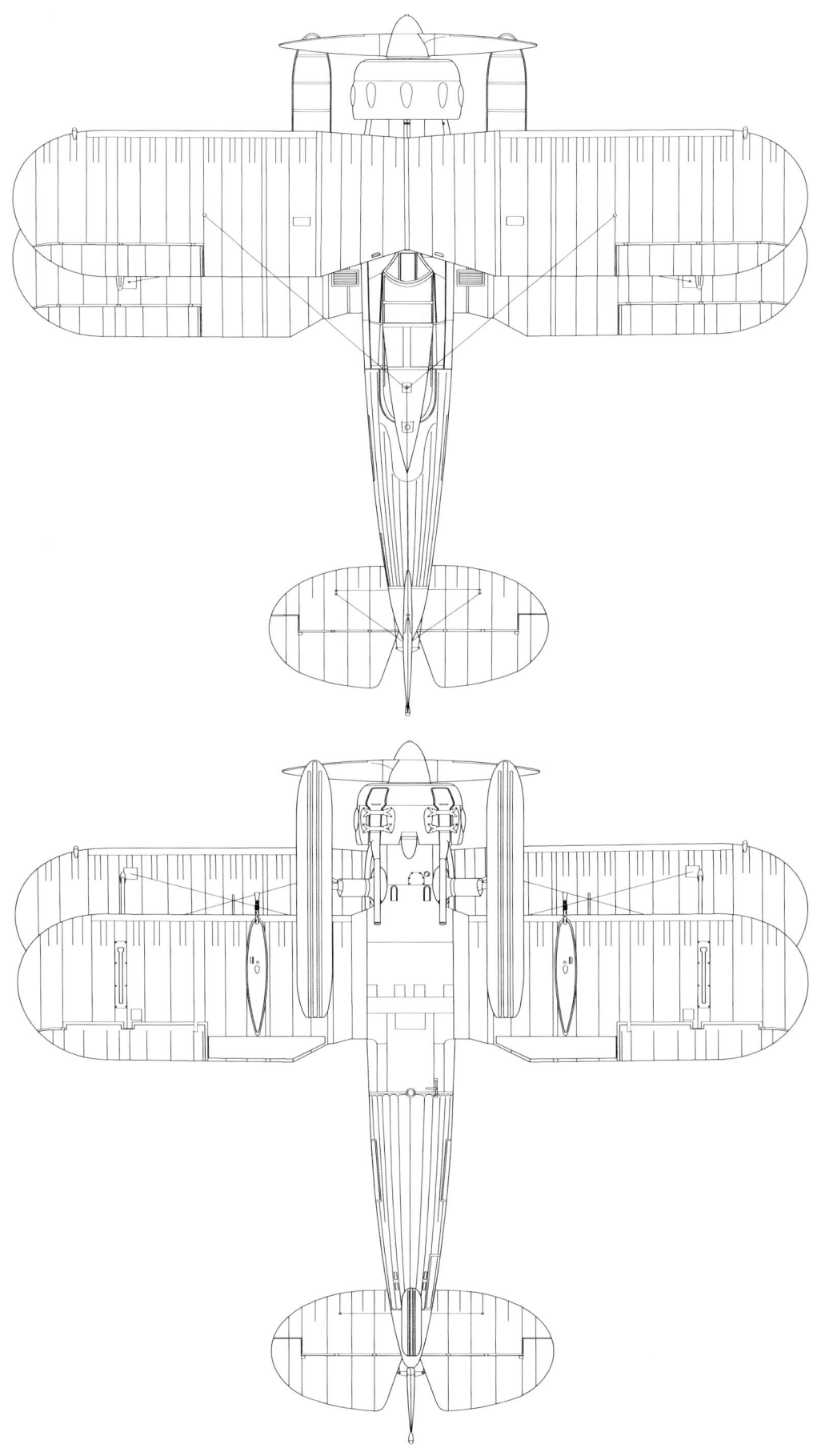

1/72

Drawings: Dariusz Karnas

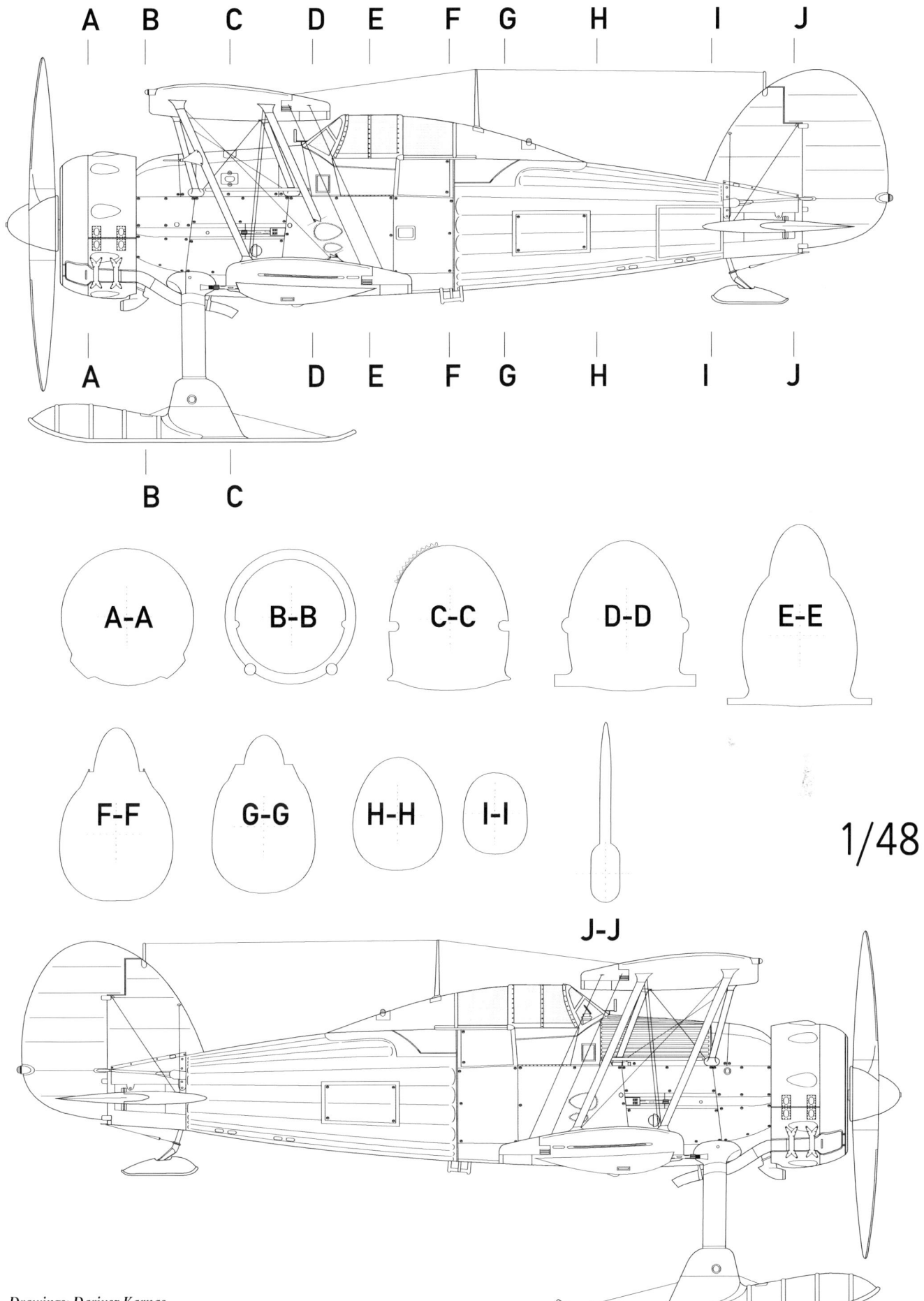

A   B   C   D   E   F   G   H   I   J

A   D   E   F   G   H   I   J

B   C

A-A   B-B   C-C   D-D   E-E

F-F   G-G   H-H   I-I   J-J

1/48

Drawings: Dariusz Karnas

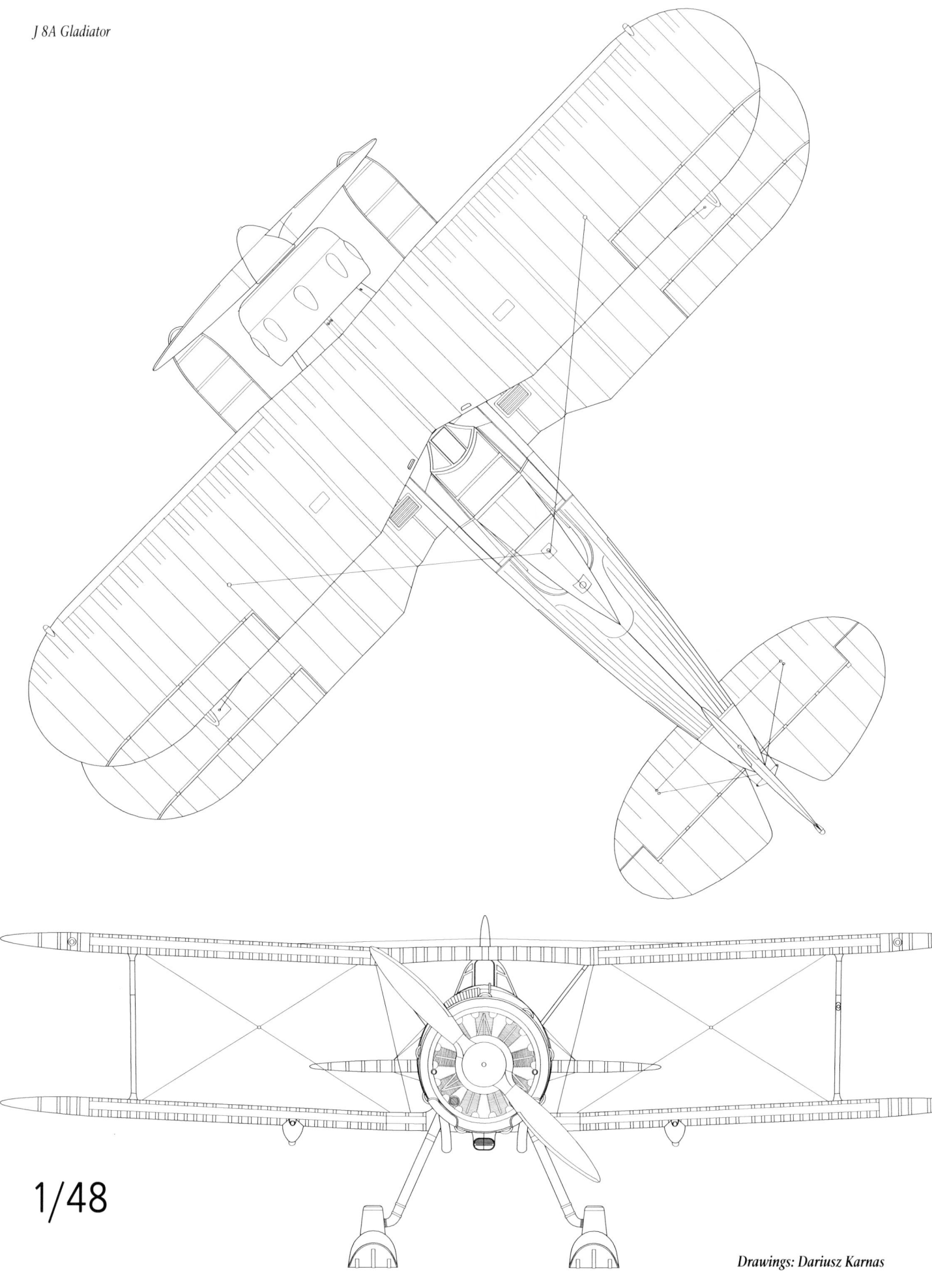

1/48

Drawings: Dariusz Karnas

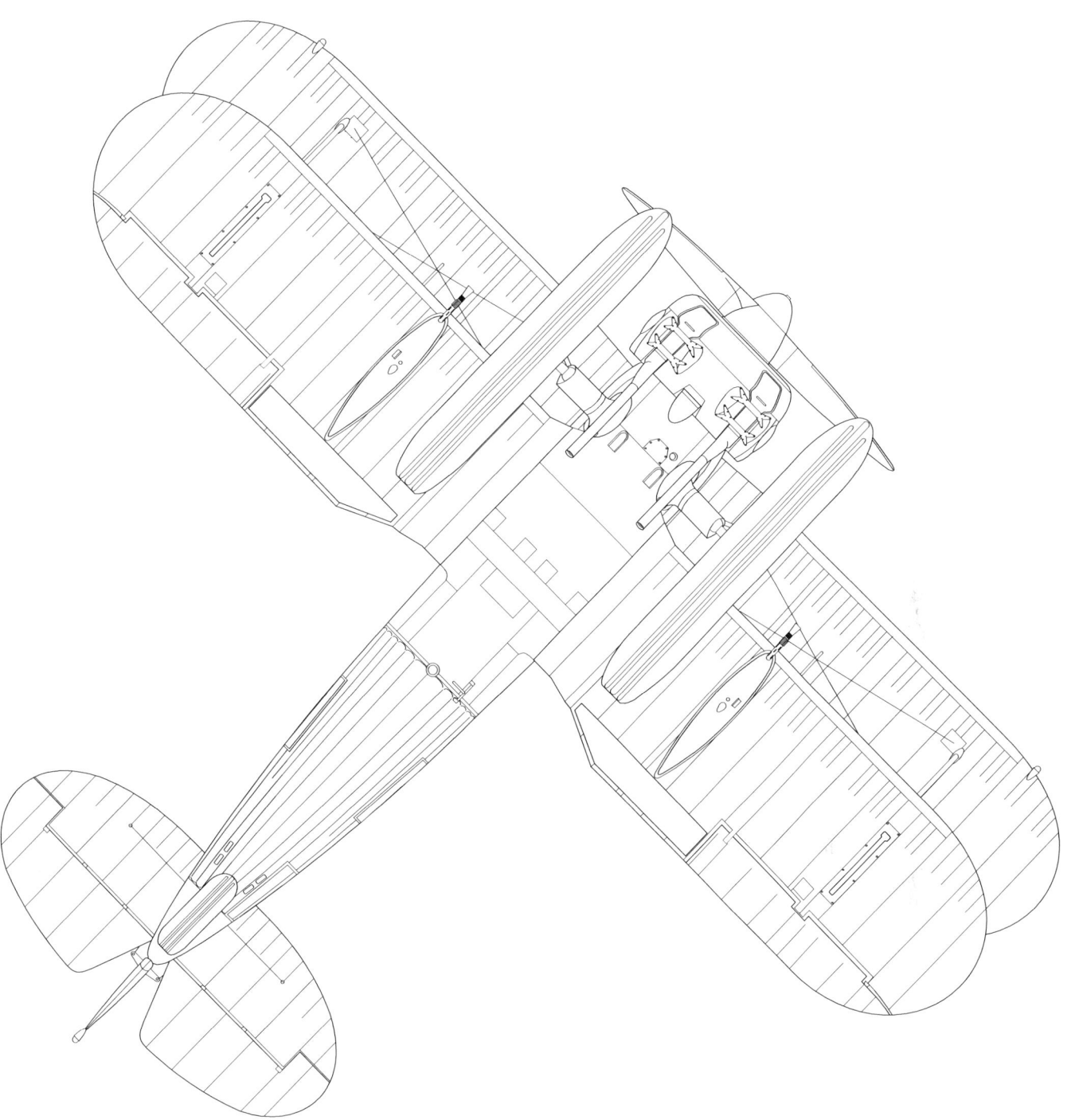

1/48

Drawings: Dariusz Karnas

Drawings of the Gloster Gladiator details published in the Flight magazine before WW2.

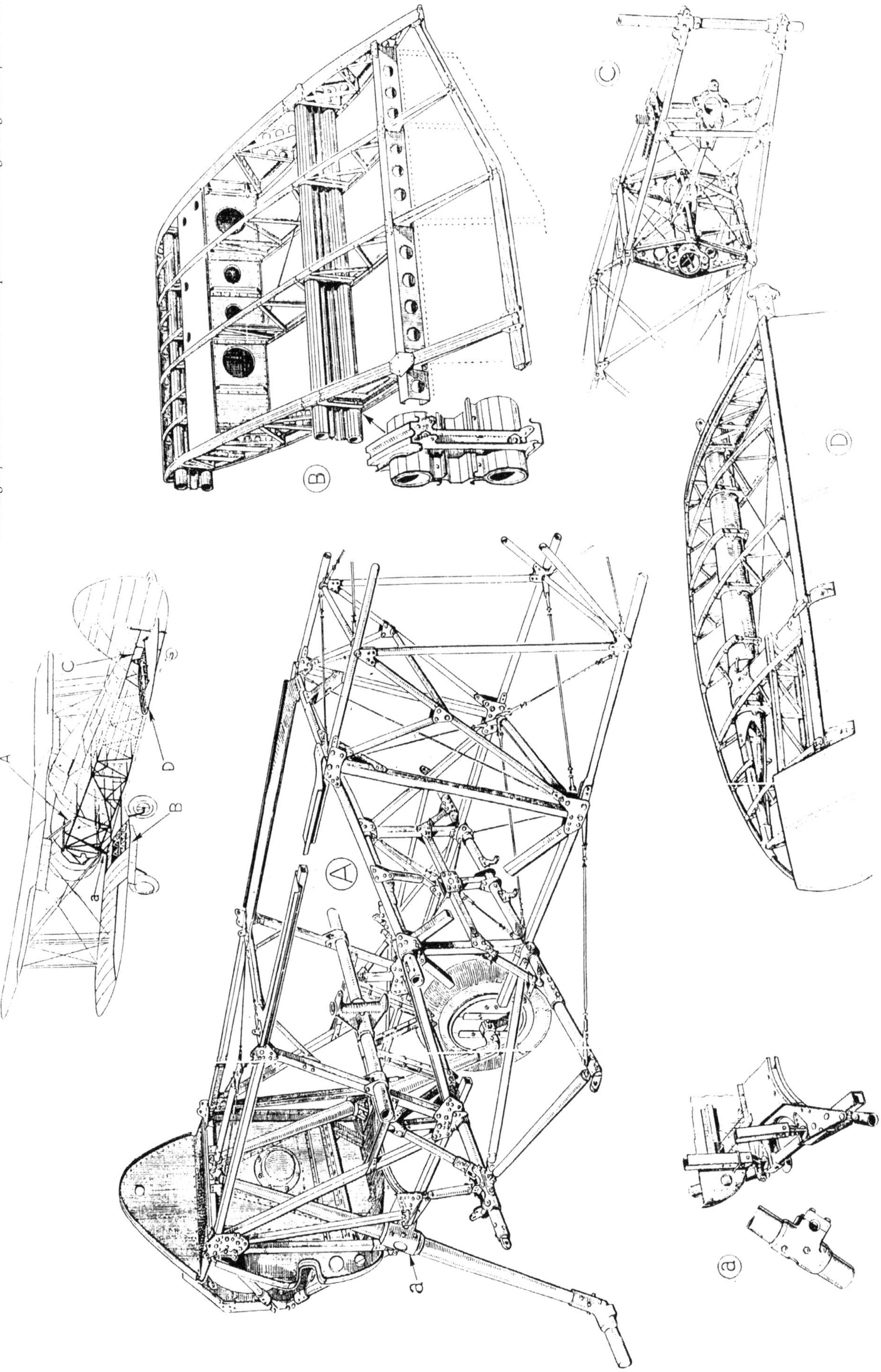

A nice underside views of a J8A no. 48 (s/n 278). It's possible this is an F8 machine from Barkarby. Photos were taken probably in 1939.
(Both Archive Svensk Flyghitorisk Förening)

J 8A no. 25 of F 9 over Gotland during the summer of 1940. (Fred Lambert-Meullers coll. via Leif Hellström)

Port side of the J 8A no. 41 (s/n 271). (via Pelle Lindqvist)

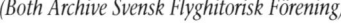

Above: Rear view, starboard side of the J 8A no. 45.

Below: With the side panels removed access to the interior of the Gladiator is very easy. The galley oil cooler can be seen below the machine gun trough. The ammo stowage bin for the fuselage machine gun is also visible.

(Both Archive Svensk Flyghitorisk Förening)

Port side of the J8A fuselage. Two tear-drop machine gun fairings are visible.
Venturi tube at the port side. Details of the centre strut and bracing are visible.
(Both photos B. Belcarz)

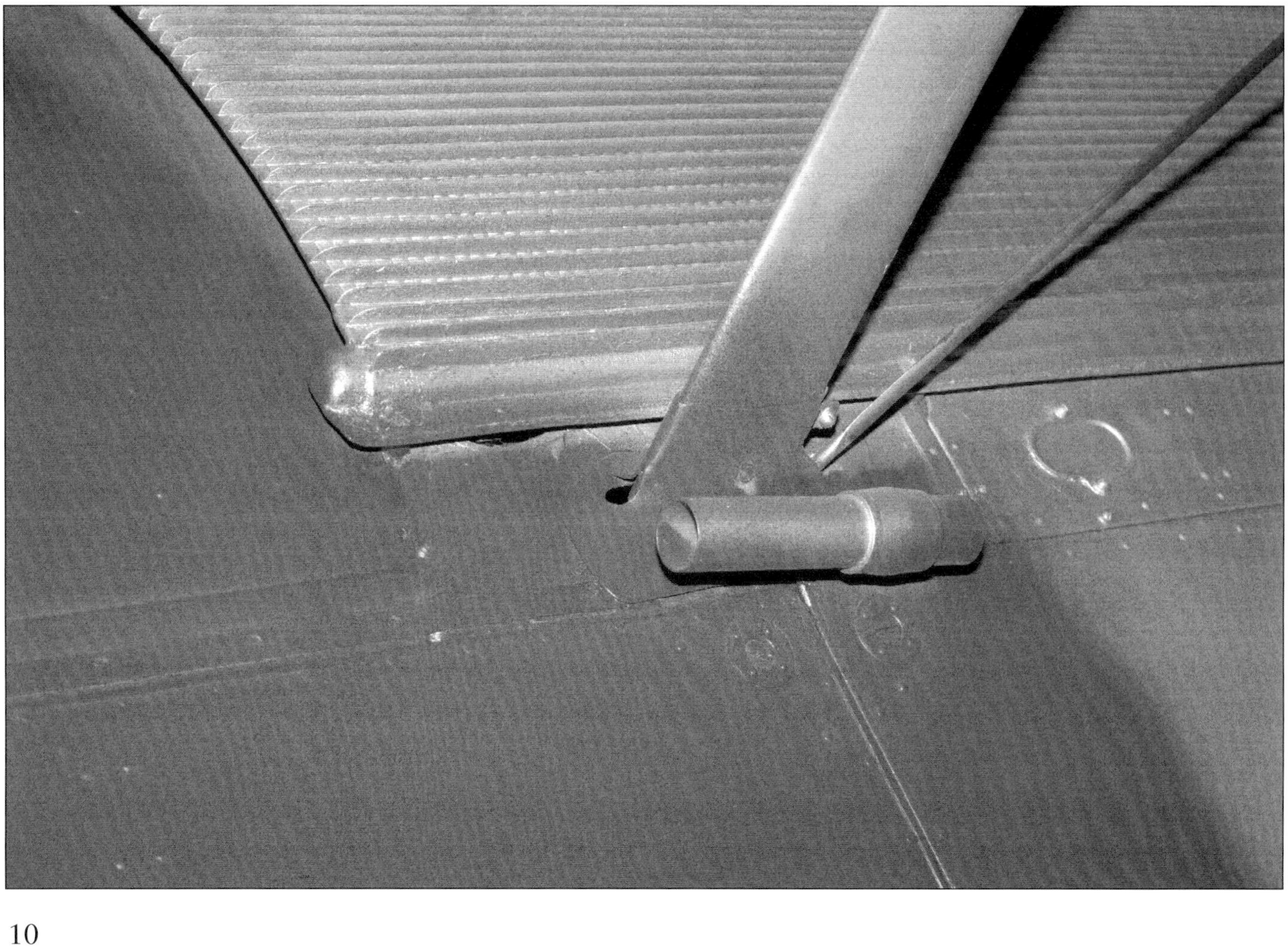

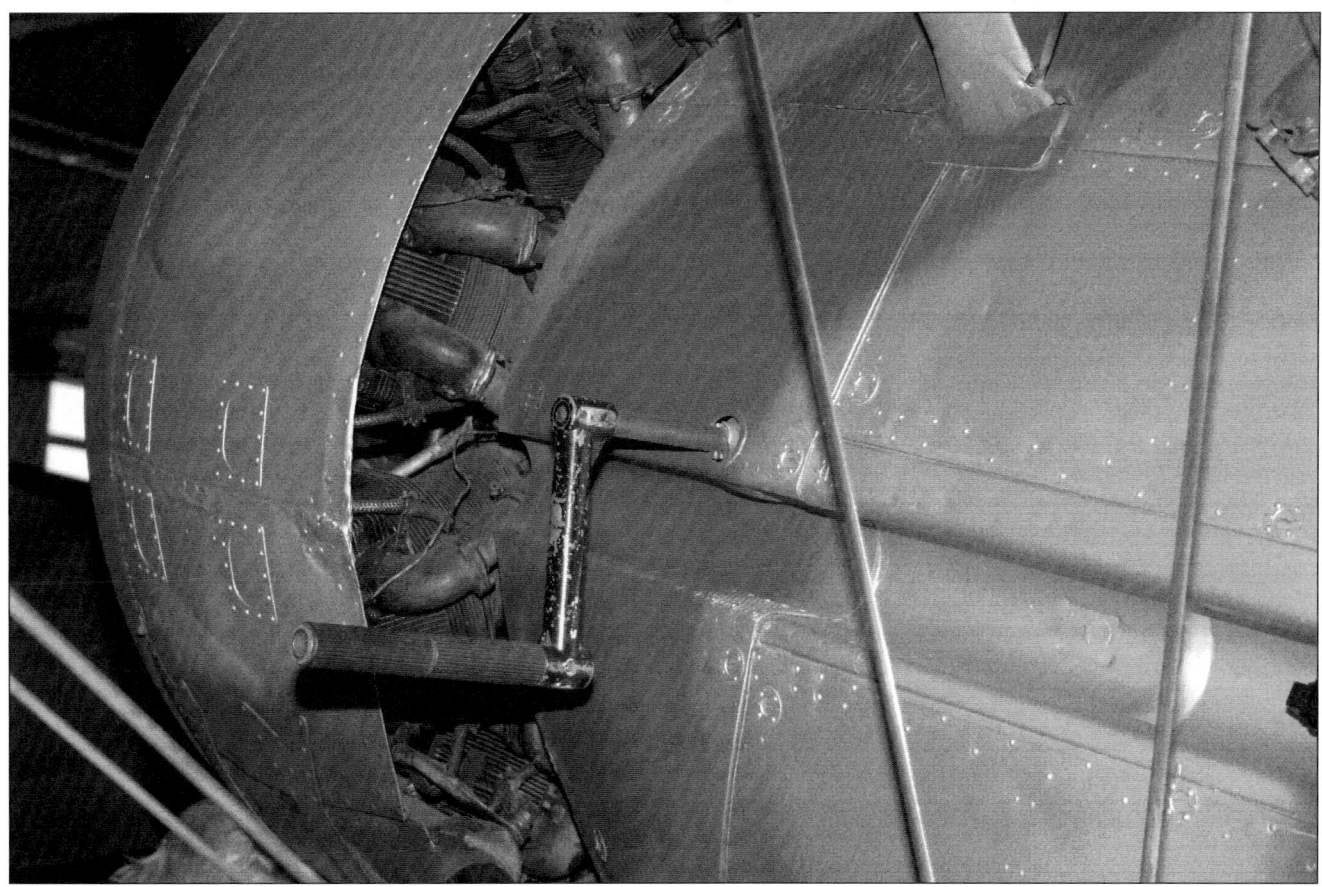

Period photo of starboard side of the J 8A. Two tear-drop machine gun fairings are visible. Note also additional hole in front of the tear-drops. (Stratus coll.)
Rear view of the Engine cylinders. Starter crank is also visible. (B. Belcarz)

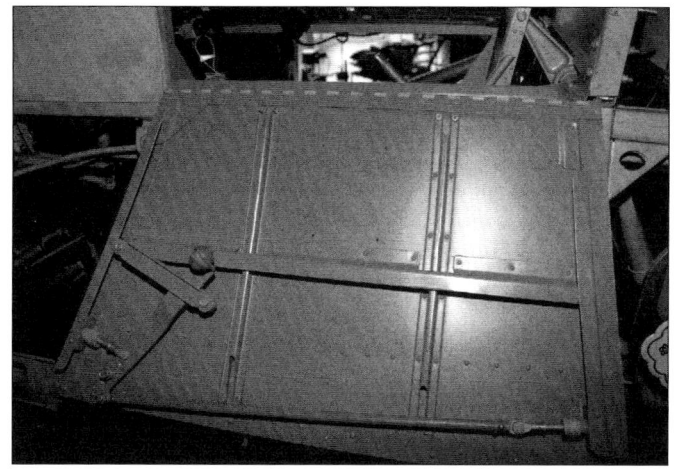 

Above: Photos of the cockpit access doors in the open position. (A. Juszczak & R. Pęczkowski)

Right: two wartime photos of the captured Gladiator. Details of the cockpit access doors are visible. (Stratus coll.)

12

Above, left: Engine cowling and the two-blade airscrew. Spinner is removed. (B. Belcarz)

Above: Detail shot of the Swedish style carburettor air intake. (B. Belcarz)

Left: Two photos of the exhaust pipes and their mount. (R. Pęczkowski)

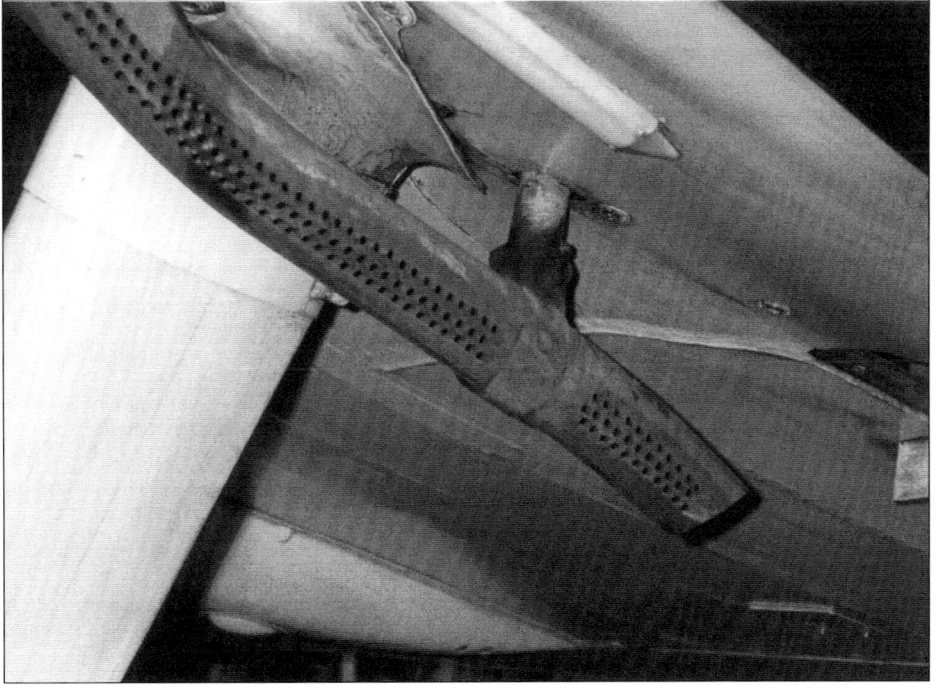

Below: The two-blade airscrew. Spinner is removed. (B. Belcarz)

13

Details of the fuselage construction, with the control cables visible.
(All photos R. Pęczkowski)

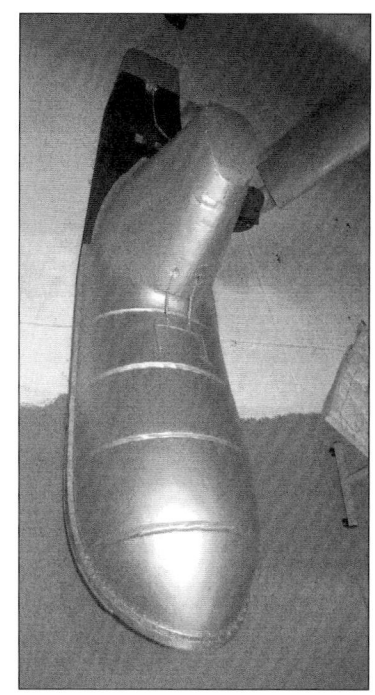

Main undercarriage of the Swedish J 8A. (All photos B. Belcarz)

Photos showing details of the tail ski. (B. Belcarz)

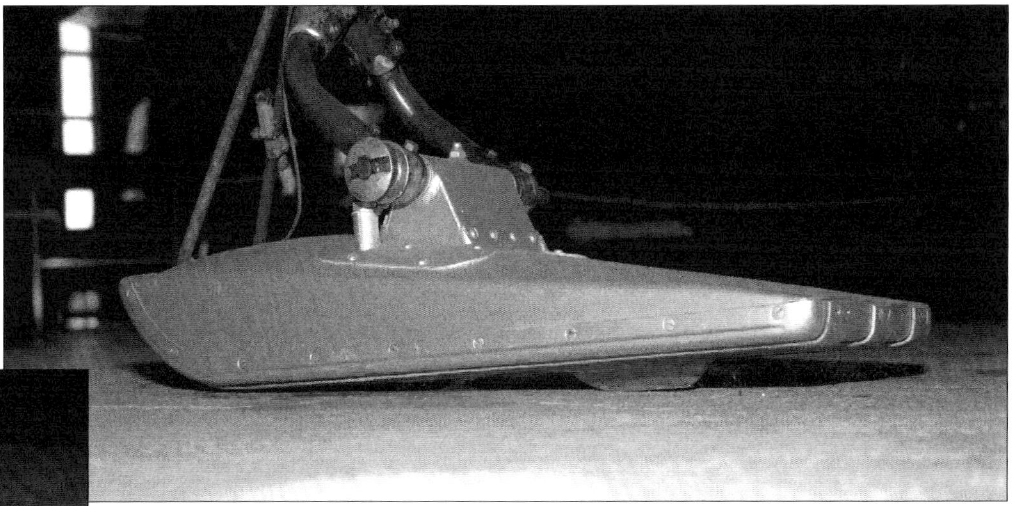

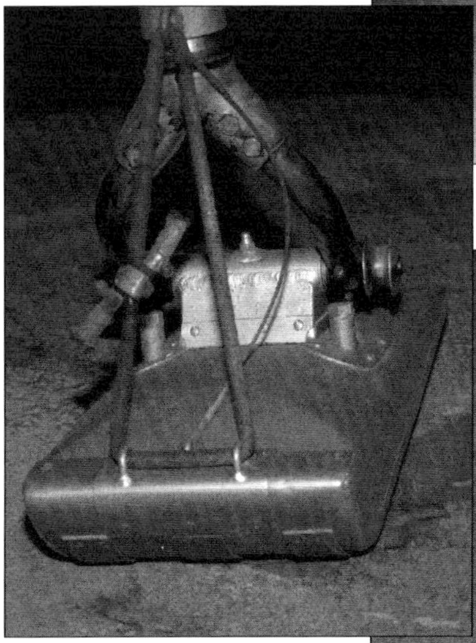

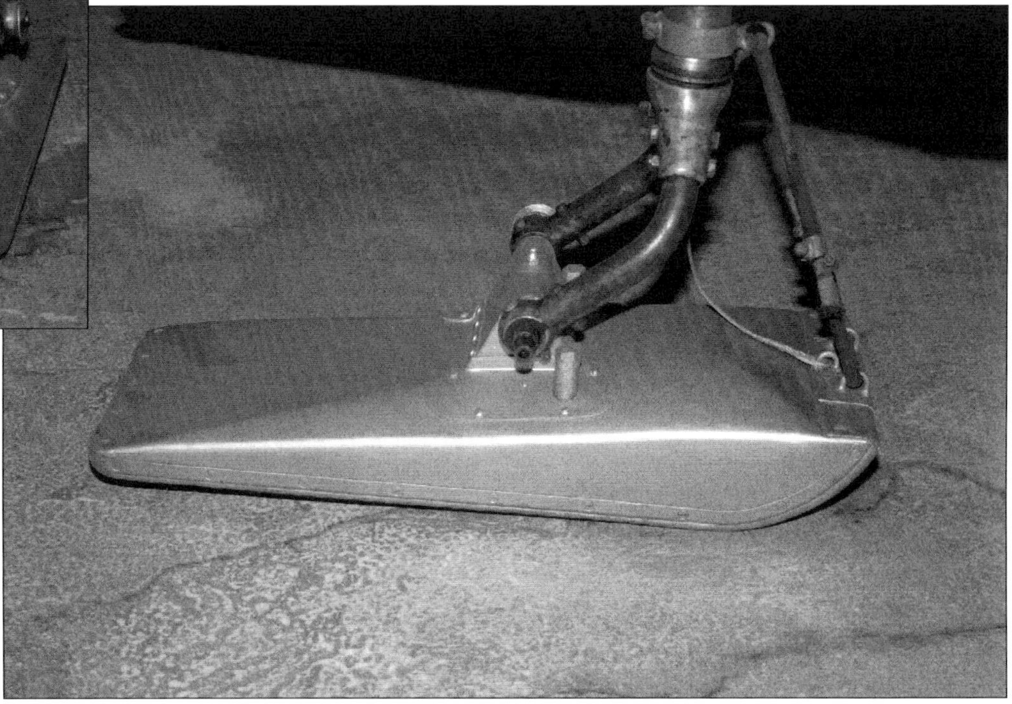

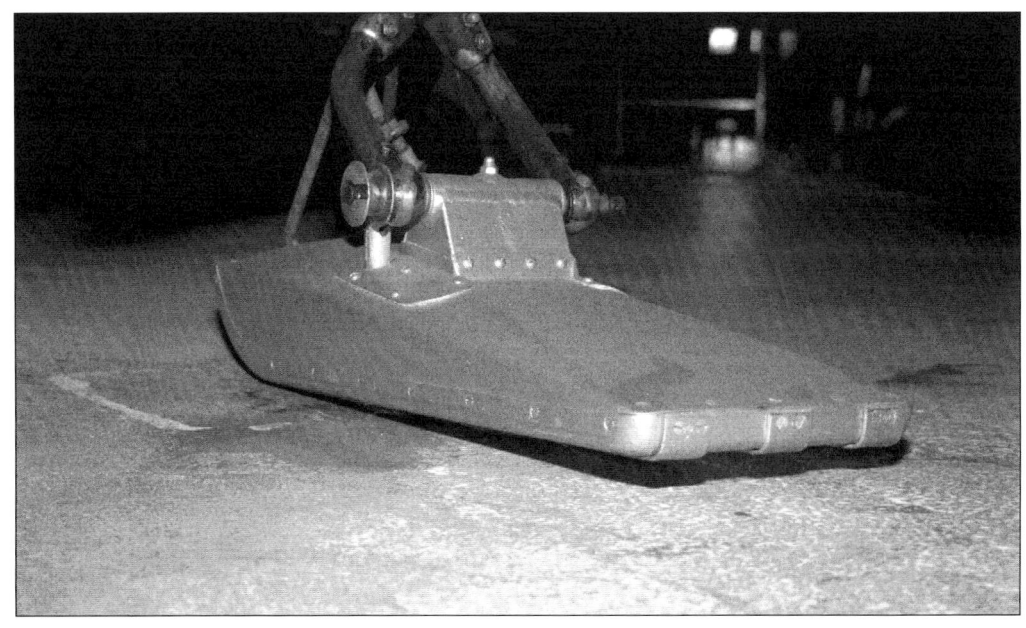

Above: Gladiator A of F 19, well camouflaged by white sheets in a temporary shelter in any of half a dozen forward bases in Lapland, between mid-January and mid-March 1940. (Mikael Forslund coll.)

Below: Gladiator A of F 19 at Kauhava on 30 March 1940. The national insignias were painted over for return to Sweden. The characters chosen showed contemporary Swedish military humour. Notice how the aluminium dope was sprayed also across the colour demarcation line. (Finnish Air Force)

Two photos of the Gladiator A of F 19 with the devil figure Sammy, after the pilot vänr.Åke Nettelbladt-Hollsten. The airmen are gunners of the same unit, at left Martin Sundsten and Thure Hansson. (Both Mikael Forslund)

Below: *Another photo of the J 8A A after return to Sweden. (Stratus coll.)*

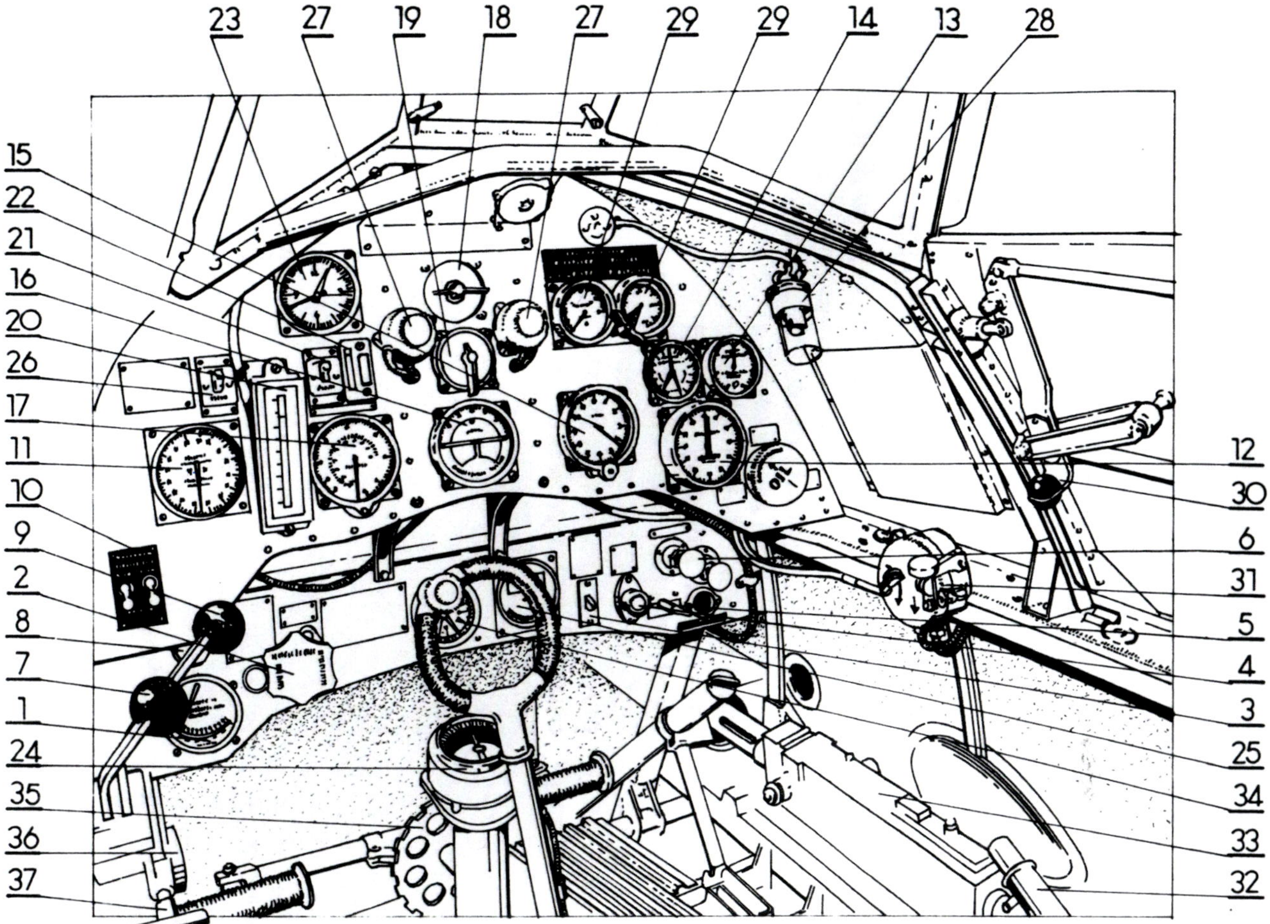

J 8A instrument panel.

1. Fuel level indicator;
2. Fuel valve;
3. Magneto switch;
4. Starter;
5. Main switch;
6. Injection pump switch;
7. Fuel mixture adjustment;
8. Fuel shut-off valve;
9. Adjusting the fuel mixture supply;
10. Generator switches;
11. Tachometer;
12. Manometer;
13. Oil pressure indicator;
14. Oil temperature indicator;
15. Altimeter;
16. Artificial horizon;
17. Airspeed indicator;
18. Vacuum regulator;
19. Three-way valve;
20. Fore-and-aft level;
21. Pitot tube temperature gauge;
22. Pitot tube gauge;
23. Clock;
24. Compass;
25. Direction indicator;
26. Exterior light switch;
27. Instrument panel light switch;
28. Cockpit light switch;
29. Oxygen indicator (pressure and supply);
30. Door lock;
31. Telegraph key;
32. Pilot's seat lever;
33. Machine gun;
34. Brake fluid pressure gauge;
35. Rudder pedals regulator;
36. Fuel supply regulator;
37. Heating regulator.

The control-rod runs of the engine controls, RAF version. (A. Juszczak)

Two photos of the Gloster J 8A Fv278 preserved at the Flygvapenmuseum (Swedish Air Force Museum) Linköping. (Both photos B. Belcarz)

Above: *Port side of the engine cowling. Swedish style carburettor air intake is clearly visible.*

Below: *Rear view of the Gloster J 8A Fv278 preserved at the Flygvapenmuseum (Swedish Air Force Museum) Linköping. (Both photos B. Belcarz)*

J 8A Gloster Gladiator, aircraft A, Flygflottilj 19, Veitsiluoto ice base, March 1940. Camouflage colours: upper surfaces Oljvgrön, under surfaces Ljust blå-grå, aluminium dope stripes. Tail letter Yellow, skis aluminium dope, spinner tip Yellow.

Karolina Hołda

Karolina Holda

J 8A Gloster Gladiator, aircraft A, Flygflottilj 19, Kauhava airfield, March 1940. Camouflage colours: upper surfaces Olivgrön, under surfaces Ljust blå-grå, aluminium dope stripes.

Starboard side emblem.

Port side emblem.

J 8A Gloster Gladiator, aircraft A, Flygflottilj 19, Kauhava airfield, March 1940.

Karolina Hołda